The Magic
Principality

The Magic Principality

A Pocket Guide to Monaco-Monte Carlo

An Eringer Travel Guide

Bartleby Press

Silver Spring, Maryland

Cover: "View from Hotel de Paris"
by Duane Alt

Eringer Travel Guides
Bartleby Press
11141 Georgia Avenue
Silver Spring, Maryland
(800) 448-1076

Library of Congress Cataloging-in-Publication Data

The magic principality : a pocket guide to Monaco-
Monte Carlo.
    p. cm.
    "An Eringer travel guide."
    ISBN 0-910155-30-5
    1. Monaco—Guidebooks. 2. Monte-Carlo
(Monaco)—Guidebooks.
    DC945.M25 1994
    916.404'5—dc20
                         94-2632
                         CIP

Manufactured in the United States of America.

Contents

Monaco
Myth and Reality

The Principality of Monaco conjures up diamond-studded, gold gilt imagery: A mosaic of princes and princesses, black-tie galas, high-stakes gambling, custom-made yachts, and Grand Prix racing.

It is a paradise to the rich and famous—a cross between Disney and Dynasty.

But it is also an ideal tourist destination for singles, couples and families seeking sun and fun, sport and culture, excellent cuisine, and the charm of the French Riviera, Europe's most beautiful coastline.

An absence of up-to-date tourist materials in English has perpetuated out-dated myths about the Principality.

Roughly the size of Central Park, Monaco is one of the great survivors of history. While the rest of Europe has seen regimes come and go, often with brutality, Monaco has been ruled—more or less peaceably—by the same royal family for almost 700 years.

And in this era of mounting national deficits, Monaco is a rare success story. It has no natural resources, yet its 30,000 citizens and residents live in comfort without having to pay income tax.

Monaco is a dynamic city-state, rushing into the 21st century with the clear focus that only a tiny country with streamlined leadership can achieve. It is Europe's real magical kingdom, a clean, unchaotic, unusually safe community, ruled by a hard-working Sovereign.

In this guide, we will strip away the myths and shed light on the facts that make Monaco a fascinating vacation spot, and an ideal base for touring the French Riviera and southern Europe.

MYTH #1: Monaco is only for millionaires.

Wrong! Though a week in a chandeliered suite at a five-star deluxe hotel can cost a as much as a new car, Monaco has a handful of cheerful hotels whose well-kept rooms are priced as low as $30 a night. And in contrast to the three-star Louis XV Restaurant's $500 dinner-for-two, the Principality abounds with family-run bistros and brasseries, where a three-course meal can cost under $20.

Myth #2: Monte Carlo is all there is to Monaco.

Absolutely not! Monte Carlo—site of the Casino and the imposing Hotel de Paris—is only *one* of Monaco's lively neighborhoods. The Palace, the Cathedral and major museums are on "The Rock" or *Monaco Ville*; the Exotic Gardens are located in

Moneghetti; the Sport Stadium and the Princess Grace Rose Garden in *Fontvieille*, the new quarter; *La Condamine*, the native harborside, has become a focal point among Monaco's young adults because of its trendy bars and restaurants.

MYTH #3: Monaco is only for gamblers.

These days, barely four percent of Monaco's income is derived from gambling. Visitors come for Monaco's well-regulated gaming, but they also come for its beaches, sporting events and its entertainment.

MYTH #4: Monaco is not for children.

Wrong again! With its plentiful playgrounds and pools, the world-class Oceanographic Museum, and a museum of mechanical toys and dolls, Monaco is a delight for children. Each winter, Monaco holds a week-long International Circus Festival; in spring, a Festival of Magic; in summer, there are spectacular firework shows twice a week; in November, the city hosts a three-week portside fun-fair. Parents will also appreciate that Monaco is exceptionally well-policed and virtually crime-free.

MYTH #5: Monaco is too isolated to serve as a vacation base.

Not so! Monaco is on the edge of Provence, within one hour's drive of Antibes and Saint Paul de Vence, the towns of Cannes and Nice, the medieval fortress at Eze, the artist's colony at Biot, and the luxury resort of Saint-Jean-Cap-Ferrat. Alpine ski slopes are within two-hours drive; the Italian Riviera is barely 20 minutes from Monte Carlo.

MYTH #6: Monaco is only for jet-setting insiders. Well, that was true...until now! Our Pocket Guide to Monaco will tell you everything you need to know about mining gold in one square mile of solid rock called Monaco.

A Brief History

*T*wenty-five hundred years ago a Ligurian tribe, the Monoikos, inhabited the hilltop plateau of old Monaco, now known as "The Rock."

Its strategic setting, 200-feet straight up, did not prevent their defeat at the hands of Augustus Caesar's Roman troops in 14 B.C.

With permission from German Emperor Henry VI, the city-state of Genoa took control of Monaco in 1191, immersing it into the perennial rivalry between two medieval political parties, the Guelphs (supporters of the Pope) and the Ghibellines (followers of the Hohenstaufen Emperor).

The Genovese fortress erected on the Rock in 1215, by Fulvio del Castello, was a Ghibelline stronghold. On January 8th, 1297, a Guelph lord, Francois (known as "Malizia" or "the spiteful") Grimaldi snuck into the fortress disguised as a Franciscan monk. No one noticed that he wore army boots instead of humble Franciscan sandals. Francois Grimaldi opened the castle gates and lead his troops to victory, expelling the resident

Spinola family and declaring itself independent of Genoa.

The Monaco Coat of Arms today displays two booted monks brandishing swords. Some believe that "Monaco" is derived not from the Monoikos, but from a derivative of Monachus, the Latin word for monk.

The dynasty started by Rainier the First has ruled Monaco for nearly 700 years. The sand-colored palace inhabited by his descendants is built on the foundations of the original thirteenth century Genovese fortress.

Monaco through the French Revolution

Due to a temporary decline in the fortunes of the Guelph party, the Grimaldis briefly lost their Monaco stronghold in 1301. Rainier's son, Charles I, regained control in 1334 and purchased the surrounding agricultural towns of Roquebrune and Menton, stretching five miles to the east, and these were linked with Monaco until the mid-1860s.

Monaco's independence was finally recognized in 1489 by Charles III, King of France. Its medieval history was bloodied by fratricides and frequent assassinations, and it alternated alliances between France and Spain, playing one against the other for protection, ensuring its survival.

Soon after the French Revolution, in 1793, France annexed Monaco and re-named it Fort Hercules. The Palace was converted into a military hospital and Honore II's magnificent art collection was auctioned. Reigning Prince Honore III was arrested in Paris with his son, the Duke of Valentinois, who later fought in Napoleon's army and campaigned for Monaco's autonomy. After the 1815 Treaty of Paris restored Monaco's sovereignty, the Treaty of Vienna divided Monaco from France and placed it under the "protection" of Sardinia, whom Monaco had fought for centuries. Sardinia exploited the Principality, and it declined under its guardianship.

Monaco's Belle Epoque

In the mid-1850s, France helped Austria defeat Sardinia, and was rewarded with the return of its southern territory. Monaco, again, became a protectorate of France, but without Menton and Rocquebrune, both of which voted for union with France. In return for allowing these two towns to secede from the Principality, France paid Monaco's Prince Charles III four million francs' compensation.

The new treaty chased out the Sardinians and reaffirmed Monaco as a sovereign state, but left Charles III without arable land and in a quandary about an alternative source of income for Monaco. Up until then, its income was derived from the sale of lemons, oranges and olive oil from the orchards of Menton and Roquebrune.

Charles III feared that poverty would turn his subjects against him, and that they might vote for a union with France. He turned to tourism: Every winter, nearby Cannes and Nice were flooded with free-spending Russian Dukes, American millionaires and English aristocrats who came to savor the balmy Mediterranean breezes. But Monaco—a four-hour horse and buggy ride on perilous mountain roads—was cut off from the gilded cash flow.

Charles III reasoned that independence made it possible to institute gambling, illegal in France. Enthused by France's pledge to run its railroad to Monaco, Charles opened a casino in La Condamine, behind the harbor, then moved it to a building across from the palace on The Rock. It did poorly, and Charles sent his private secretary to Hamburg, a German gambling resort, to lure gaming promoter Francois Blanc to Monaco.

Known as "The Wizard" in gaming circles, Francois Blanc moved to the Principality in 1863 and was awarded a fifty-year franchise to promote the Societe Anonyme des Bains de Mer et du Cercle des Etrangers, known best by its acronym, SBM.

There were reasons for this long-winded name: The euphemistic label of a "Sea Bathing Association" gave a respectable gloss to the resort's breadwinner: the Casino. (Sea-bathing was considered a "cure," not a pleasure in the mid-19th century.) The reference to a "Foreigner's Club" was apropos because the Casino was (and still is) off-limits to all Monegasques, a paternalistic decree intended to keep Monaco's citizens from ruining themselves financially at the gaming tables.

In return for the gambling monopoly granted to it, SBM took responsibility for the Principality's public services, transforming Monaco, effectively, into a "corporate state."

After briefly considering the name "Albertville" for the new gambling resort on the Speluges plateau, Charles named it after himself—Monte Carlo ("Mount Charles").

The Hotel de Paris, built to accommodate gamblers, was opened in 1864. The completion of the Nice-Menton railroad in 1868 delivered flocks of rich and titled visitors to Monaco. A year later, the Prince's bankroll was so large that he abolished direct taxation.

Nice, envious of Monaco's right to gambling, threatened to march on the Principality after the French Government upheld Charles III's right to sovereignty in 1870. Francois Blanc closed the Casino. Shamefaced, Nice's prefecture asked that the Casino be reopened because Nice's own hotels—now dependent on Monaco tourism—were afraid of going bankrupt.

In 1871, 140,000 tourists visited Monaco, and the Casino took in five million gold francs. The saga of modern Monaco had begun.

Twentieth Century Monaco

Prince Albert I succeeded his father in 1889. A gifted marine explorer, Albert sailed the world, and founded Monaco's Oceanographic Institute which, under Jacques Cousteau direction, was put on the cutting edge of marine biological research. Its museum is one of Monaco's chief tourist attractions.

A Constitution was adopted in 1911. And the Monte Carlo Rally was launched, to be followed

17 years later by the Grand Prix, Monaco's premier sporting event.

At this time, Monaco's peak season was winter, from December to March. Before the First World War, foreigners rarely visited the Riviera in the summer. Bathing in the sea, let alone in the sun, was practically unknown. The Principality was a favorite destination of Russian Grand Dukes, who took 48-hour train-journeys to the sunshine of the Mediterranean to escape the harsh winters of St. Petersburg.

Monaco stayed neutral in World War I, but Albert's son, Prince Louis II, fought with France, and Monaco's grand hotels were converted to hospitals. Between the wars, Prince Louis created the Saint-Roman tennis courts, the Monte Carlo Beach Club and the Sporting d'Ete, an entertain-

---

Titles Galore

Throughout centuries of advantageous marriages to noble heirs and heiresses, the Grimaldis have accumulated a plethora of secondary aristocratic titles: Duke de Valentinois, Marquis des Baux, Count de Calardez, Baron de Buis, Sire de Matignon, Seigneur de Saint-Remy, Count de Torrigni, Baron de Rambye, Baron de la Luthmiere, Duke de Mazarin, Baron d'Altkirch, Prince de Chateau-Porcier, Marquis de Chilly, Baron de Massy, Marquis de Guiscard.

The motto on the Grimaldi coat of arms is "Deo Juvanti"—Latin for "With God's Help."

ment complex. In 1936 the state relieved SBM of its responsibility for the management of Monaco's public services.

During World War II, Monaco was occupied by the Italians, then the Germans; Hereditary Prince Rainier, Louis's grandson, fought with the French.

Prince Rainier III, son of Princess Charlotte and Prince Pierre, de Polignac, succeeded to the throne on Louis' death in 1949. Prince Rainier's fairytale marriage in 1956 to Hollywood actress Grace Patricia Kelly produced three heirs: Princess Caroline Louise Marguerite (1957); Hereditary Prince Albert Alexandre Louis Pierre (1958) and Princess Stephanie Marie Elisabeth (1965). The accidental death of Princess Grace in 1982 was mourned throughout the world.

During his reign, now in its 44th year, Prince Rainier has transformed Monaco from a gambling resort into a sporting, cultural and commercial center, dramatically expanding its territory with daring land reclamation projects.

Hard Facts

Son Monaco suora uno scoglio
Non semino ne raccoglio
Eppur mangia voglio!

> *I am Monaco, on a rock so steep*
> *That I don't sow and I don't reap*
> *But nonetheless, I still want to eat!*

*T*his traditional Monegasque rhyme accur-
ately sums up the Principality's economic
situation for much of its existence: no arable
terrain, no natural resources. In the late 1800s
Charles III realized Monaco's only assets—
sunshine, beaches, and the right to establish
gambling—to create an income based on tourism.
When first created, SBM generated 95 percent of
Monaco's treasury revenue.

Today SBM is a quasi-public company, partly
traded on the Paris stock exchange and controlled
by Monaco's government. It remains the Principality's largest employer and its enterprises occupy

almost one-twelfth of Monaco's land area. But SBM is no longer the State's sole supporter. Gambling concessions account for only 4.3 percent of Monaco's income. (That said, slot machines alone rake in 35 million francs a year!)

In fact, Monaco's tourism accounts for only one-quarter of the Principality's revenues. (Year-round occupancy of Monaco's hotels averages 70 percent.)

So what accounts for the Principality's extra-ordinary prosperity, and an annual turnover that has escalated from 3.25 billion francs in 1975 to 25.4 billion francs in 1989?

Banking

With 57 banks in the Principality, and many more setting up shop early this decade, the money-spinner in Monaco is money itself. Financial institutions from the world over wave their banners in Monaco to take advantage of relatively relaxed tax laws, and to offer banking facilities to the mega-wealthy who make Monaco their legal domicile.

Monaco has no personal income tax, no capital gains tax, and no property tax.

Industry

Industry represents 25.5 percent of the commerce conducted in Monaco. There are over seven hundred active companies in the Principality. (Unlike tax-havens, Monaco does not permit companies "on paper."). These range from LANCASTER, an international cosmetics firm, to LA MONEGASQUE, the world's largest anchovy processor.

Demographics

Of the 29,972 residents (1990 census), only 5,070 are native Monegasques. They benefit from a host of privileges, including rent-controlled housing and free medical care. There is no military conscription; Monaco's police and carabinieri, which doubles as a militia, must be French, a law decreed a century ago to prevent a Monegasque-inspired coup d'etat.

25,000 foreign residents from 100 countries have created a jet-set melting pot. Its celebrity residents include Boris Becker, Karl Lagerfeld, Ringo Starr, Sean Connery, Shirley Bassey, Luciano Pavarotti and Placido Domingo.

A University in Monaco

The University of Southern Europe (USE), founded in 1986, is a private business and finance school situated in Fontvieille. It offers an American-style undergraduate curriculum, and a BS degree in Business Administration. Courses are taught in English.

> 2, avenue Prince Hereditaire Albert
> MC 98000 Monaco
>
> Tel. 92.05.70.57

The French are the most numerous (12,047), followed by the Italians (5,000).

Conditions to establish legal domicile in Monaco are straightforward: One must own or rent an apartment in the Principality, provide proof of financial independence, and spend at least half the year in residence.

Monegasque nationality is rarely granted and requires a recommendation from the Prince's Council.

Government

The Principality has been a hereditary constitutional monarchy since 1911. The crown passes through direct primogeniture, with preference for male heirs. The Prince serves as chief of state, advised by a Crown Council, comprised of Monegasques.

Monegasques vote to fill the 18-member National Council (which makes laws) and the 15-member Municipal Council (which appoints a mayor from within its ranks).

Monaco enjoys a close political relationship with France. Its chief civil servant, the Minister of State, is appointed by the Prince from a list of three French candidates presented him by the French government; a three-member Council of State is chosen jointly by the Prince and the French government. Other key posts, such as the chief of police and chief justice of the Supreme Court are also filled by the French.

France is protector of Monaco's independence

and territorial integrity, and the Principality must act in accordance with the interests of France.

Monaco belongs to many international organizations, including UNESCO, the World Health Organization, and the International Red Cross.

In 1993 Monaco was admitted as a full member to the United Nations.

Logistics

Before You Go

A valid passport is required. A visa is unnecessary for visits up to 90 days.

There are three Monaco Tourist Offices in the US:

New York City: 845 Third Avenue 10022
Tel. (212) 759-6227

Chicago: 542 S. Dearborn Street 60605
Tel. (312) 939-7863

La Jolla, CA: 1001 Genter Street, Suite 4E
Tel. (619) 459-4320

Getting There

By Air:
Nice-Cote d'Azur International Airport is 15 miles west of Monaco.

Delta is the only carrier that operates nonstop flights between the USA and Nice (from both New York and Atlanta); daily during peak summer season, three times a week off-season. Flight time: Eight to nine hours.

TWA offers a daily direct flight from New York to Nice via Barcelona.

Air France and several American airlines fly nonstop from many US cities to Paris. Air France and Air Inter have flights throughout the day from Paris to Nice (75 minutes).

Air France (800) 237-2747; Local: 93.18.89.89
Delta (800) 221-1212; Local: 05.35.40.80
TWA (800) 221-2000; Local: 93.21.45.90

Most European airlines fly non-stop routes connecting Nice with European capitals.

From the Airport to Monaco:

Helicopter: The fastest way is by helicopter. Heli Air Monaco can whisk you to Monaco's Fontvieille Heliport in seven minutes while providing a breathtaking view of Nice, Cap Ferrat and Beaulieu. Part of the service is a free ride from the Heliport to your destination in Monaco. At 350 francs/$64, it is less expensive for one person to take the helicopter than a taxi. You may make reservations in advance or buy a ticket upon arrival at Nice airport.

Heli Air Monaco   Tel. 92.05.00.50
Fax. 92.05.76.17

Taxi: Depending on traffic, 30 to 50 minutes. Cost: approximately 400 francs/$73. Fasten your seat belt; you might get an out-of-work rally driver with a penchant for hairpin turns.

Bus: A 70-minute ride priced at 75 francs/$13.50

By Train:
Two choices from Paris:

1. Overnight from Gare de Lyon. Departs early evening; arrives in Monaco early the next morning. A 12-hour journey.
2. The TGV (high speed train), from Paris to Nice in seven hours. Change at Nice for a local train to Monaco (20 minutes).

Trainfares vary.
Monaco's train station is located near the port.

Passenger information: 93.87.50.50
Advance bookings: 93.88.89.93

By Road:
Monaco is connected to the major cities of southern France by the A8 motorway (Monaco exit).

Three parallel roads connect Nice to Monaco: The "Basse Corniche" which hugs the coast; the "Moyen (middle) Corniche"; and the mountaintop "Grande Corniche," recommended for good drivers with adventurous spirit.

In Monaco

Currency:
Although you may occasionally handle Monegasque coins, French currency is the Principality's legal tender. Banks and Bureaux de Change offer better rates of exchange than hotels and casinos.

As currency conversions fluctuate, the dollar prices throughout this guide are approximate.

Post Office:
Monaco's main post office is in Monte Carlo, near the Grand Casino, at Palais de la Scala, Beaumarchais Square. Open Monday to Friday, 8:00 a.m. to 7:00 p.m., Saturday, 8:00 a.m. till noon.

There are subsidiary post offices in each quarter, and stamps are also available through tabac shops and most hotels. Monaco issues its own stamps; postal rates are the same as those in France. The post office has facilities for long-distance telephone calls.

Telephone:
The code to dial the US is 191 + area code + number.

To use public telephones, purchase a French Telecom phone card from local tabacs.

Language:
Most residents, shop-keepers and service personnel speak English, some more fluent than others. An attempt to speak French, the official language, is always appreciated. Conversational Italian can also be helpful. There is a traditional Monegasque language, spoken by older people, taught in schools, and still found on street signs on The Rock.

English Language Newspapers:
The *International Herald Tribune,* published six days a week, is available early every morning.

An international edition of *USA Today* is published weekdays.

An international edition of the *Wall Street Journal* (weekdays) appears early afternoon, along with an array of British newspapers, from the pink *Financial Times* to the yellow *Daily Mirror*.

On Sunday, watch the expatriate English community clamoring around the tabac at Cafe de Paris at 2:00 p.m., awaiting the arrival of the (London) *Sunday Times* and other English newspapers.

Religion:

Roman Catholicism is the state religion. The three major places of worship are:

CATHEDRAL OF MONACO
Monaco-Ville.
Tel. 93.30.87.70

SAINT-CHARLES CHURCH
avenue Saint-Charles, Monte Carlo.
Tel. 93.30 74.90

SAINT-DEVOTE CHURCH
place Saint-Devote, La Condamine
Tel. 93.50.52.60

Places of Worship for other faiths:

ANGLICAN:
Saint-Paul's Church, 22 avenue de Grande-Bretagne
Monte Carlo. Tel. 93.30.71.06

PROTESTANT:
Reformed Church, 9 rue Louis Notari, La Condamine
Tel. 93.30.29.27

JEWISH:
Synagogue and Community Center, 15 avenue de
la Costa.
Tel. 93.30.16.46

Monaco National Holidays

New Year's Day	January 1st
Saint Devote	January 27th
May Day	May 1st
Ascension Day	End of May
Assumption Day	August 15th
All Saint's Day	November 1st
The Prince's Fete	November 19th
Christmas	December 25th

Tipping

Service is generally included in the price at restaurants unless, in rare cases, otherwise stipulated. Tips, therefore, need not be given routinely, but only in appreciation of excellent service. It is considered polite, if you are pleased by your meal and the service, to leave a five-to-ten-percent gratuity.

Climate

Monaco is known for its 300 sunny days a year.

January and February are the Principality's best kept secrets. It is nearly always sunny, with temperatures reaching 60 degrees or higher. Winter was Monaco's peak season until sun-bathing became fashionable early this century.

April showers bring spring flowers.

Summer months sizzle with heat and high-volume tourism.

Some prefer the cooler, calmer months of September and October.

Getting Around in Monaco

On Foot:
You can walk everywhere in Monaco. Six public elevators take the sting out of the Principality's hilly terrain. They ascend and descend the varying levels of Monaco, which is built on the side of a French alp. Precise locations of the elevators may be found on maps of Monaco, available at all hotels and at the tourism office.

By Taxi:
You can telephone a taxi for a pick-up, 24-hour service, or grab a cab at one of several taxi stands, conveniently placed at the train station, the Casino and other easy-to-find locations.

Fares: 50 francs/$9 anywhere in the Principality.
Tel. 93.15.01.01 and 93.50.56.28

By Bus:
Monaco's small buses are comfortable and efficient. Five different routes link all major destinations. A single fare is 8½ francs/$1.35; a four-ride carnet is 17 francs; an eight-ride carnet is 28½ francs/$4.70. Buses stop running at 9:00 p.m.

Parking:
Underground parking lots abound. They are easy to use and inexpensive. Most hotels in Monte Carlo offer valet parking.

Medical Emergencies

There is always a doctor or pharmacist on duty. Simply pick up the phone and dial 141.

The Princesse Grace Hospital (MC), avenue Pasteur.

Emergencies: Tel. 93.25.98.69

Sleeping Around

*O*ver two-thirds of the 2,400-plus hotel rooms in Monaco are in four-star and four-star luxe establishments. But moderately priced, and even downright inexpensive rooms DO exist.

Rates are generally less expensive off-season (November to May).

Key:

Location symbols—

MC	Monte Carlo
C	Condamine
F	Fontvieille
MV	Monaco Ville ("The Rock")

Price categories—

$$$$	Very expensive
$$$	Expensive
$$	Moderate
$	Inexpensive

All major credit cards are accepted unless otherwise indicated.

FOUR STAR LUXE

Hotel de Paris (MC) $$$$
Place du Casino. Tel. 92.16.30.00 Fax. 93.25.59.17
Two hundred and sixty rooms, 40 suites. 24-hour room service, valet parking, swimming pool, air conditioning, three gourmet restaurants, bar, shops, travel agency, hairdresser, three conference rooms.

A visit to the Hotel de Paris is a must even if one is staying elsewhere. Its restaurants, among the finest in Europe, are covered in the next chapter. Recently modernized, this hotel blends the Belle Epoque style with comfortability.

"Price is no object," was the directive François Blanc gave his decorators in 1863 for the gilded Belle Epoque Hotel de Paris. He demanded nothing less than the grandest hotel in the world, and spared no expense to achieve this ambition.

Its roots are obviously in gambling. Room numbers with the unlucky "13" are taboo (room 212A falls between 212 and 214). It is a Monaco tradition to rub the well-worn knee of Louis XV's horse, a

---

The Hotel de Paris is SBM's flagship hotel. SBM's three other hotels are the Hermitage, the Mirabeau, and the Monte Carlo Beach Hotel. Guests at SBM hotels are issued a "Carte d'Or" (Gold Card) which accords privileged access to the Casino's private rooms, SBM nightclubs and pools, and the members-only Monaco Golf and Tennis clubs. SBM cars are available to shuttle guests from hotel to private beach.

brass equestrian statue in the center of the lobby, before heading for the Casino across the street.

Winston Churchill, in the autumn of his life, resided in this elegantly furnished hotel, and a suite still bears his name and sports a bronze bust of the English statesman by Kees Verkade.

A marble tunnel links the hotel to the "Piscine des Terrasse," a pool and spa complex overlooking the harbor.

In the 1950s, '60s, and '70s the American Bar was the focal point of Hollywood stars attracted to the Riviera by Princess Grace. On gala nights, it is an ideal people-watching spot.

Hotel Hermitage (MC) $$$$

Square Beaumarchais. Tel. 93.50.67.31 Fax. 93.50.47.12

Two hundred and sixty rooms. 24-hour room service, valet parking, swimming pool, air conditioning, piano bar, restaurant, conference rooms.

The Hermitage, built in 1900, blends neo-classic elements with the pomp that was calculated to please the free-spending Grand Dukes and Duchesses of Imperial Russia.

Built into the side of a rock, its interior is a complex maze of half-staircases and seemingly endless corridors. Aristotle Onassis used a private tunnel beneath the Hermitage terrace that linked his office to Maria Callas's groundfloor suite, now "Le Bar-Terrasse," an elegant piano bar.

Many of the rooms were recently remodeled.

A lunch or dinner in the gilt-trimmed Belle Epoque dining room is an experience for its grand decor, not, unfortunately, for its cuisine.

Loews Monte Carlo (MC) $$$$

12 avenue des Spelugues. Tel. 93.50.65.00 Fax. 93.30.01.57

US reservations: (800) 235-3697 Junkets are available for serious gamblers.

Six hundred and fifty rooms and suites. 24-hour room service, valet parking, swimming pool, fitness center, casino, four bars, six restaurants, cabaret, business center, eleven conference rooms, travel agency, car rental, shops, air conditioning, CNN.

Reputed to be the most successful convention hotel on the French Riviera, Loews is almost a resort within a resort.

It is modern, comfortable and extremely American. The ground floor Sun casino is American-style, with an emphasis on slot machines.

The expansive Piano Bar features floor to ceiling picture windows with panoramic views of the sea, the beach and Cap Martin, and pianist Vlad Farrari six nights a week (not Tuesday).

Le Pistou, a provencal theme restaurant, offers enchanting views of Monte Carlo by night. The authentic cuisine includes an hors d'ouvre of minced black olive tapenade and stuffed herb bread. Specialties include lamb roasted on the spit and a ratatouille of eggplant, zucchini and garlic.

The Spa, obsessively clean, has state-of-the-art

exercise equipment, personal trainers, tanning facilities, sauna, steamroom and jacuzzi.

The adjoining penthouse pool is heated to 82 F and its terrace offers a stunning, panoramic view.

The ground floor travel agency, Monaco Congres et Tourisme, is perhaps the most efficient in Monaco. Tel. 93.30.78.97.

Rooms are spacious, light and airy, each with a private terraced balcony or access to an open terrace.

If you are looking for European charm, this hotel is not for you. If convenience and comfortablity are your priorities, you need go no further. *Be certain to request a room overlooking the sea.*

Le Metropole Palace (MC) $$$
(check for special offers)
4 avenue de la Madone. Tel. 93.15.15.15 Fax. 93.25.24.44
One hundred and seventy rooms including 30 suites and 45 junior suites. 24-hour room service, valet parking, swimming pool, piano bar, two restaurants, air conditioning, shops, conference rooms, CNN.

A new hotel, built in Belle Epoque style, situated above the Metropole Gallerie (shopping center), a stone's throw from Place du Casino, and a favorite of Luciano Pavarotti, who has a suite named after him.

Despite its superb location, the Metropole Palace got off to a slow start, and this has caused its management to offer special deals at bargain rates, even during peak season.

Rooms are large, if oddly fitted, and the heated swimming pool with bar and terrace are blissfully quiet and peaceful all summer long, in contrast to the bustle at Loews' pool.

The Metropole's Sunday buffet brunch is popular among Monaco's elegant old-timers; it offers good value for a hearty appetite.

FOUR STAR

Monte Carlo Beach Hotel (MC) $$$
Route du Beach. Tel. 93.78.21.40
Fifty rooms. 24-hour room service, valet parking, swimming pool, solarium, private beach, bungalows, three restaurants, hairdresser, shops, conference room. Open only from mid-April through October.

Probably the most exclusive "resort" hotel in Monaco, this clubby inn is sporty and casual, completely renovated in 1993. An ochre stucco villa with tiled roof overlooking a terra cotta sundeck, an Olympic-size seawater pool and a private beach with cabanas. One of its three open-air restaurants, Le Vigie, serves a popular luncheon buffet on a deck built on the rocks.

The man with the pony tail looking down on you from the hilltop "Villa Vigie" is probably Karl Lagerfeld. This villa was gifted to fashion designer Lagerfeld by SBM for his lifetime in exchange for his restoration of it.

Guest rooms are small and simple, but the beach is THE place to bronze. Competition among Monaco's celebrity residents for summertime cabana rentals is fierce.

Not actually in Monaco, the Beach Club is across the border on land leased by France to the Principality. For this reason, a car rental would be useful if you choose this hotel for your lodging. There is, however, an SBM shuttle bus from this hotel to Place du Casino.

Hotel Mirabeau (MC) $$$
1-3 avenue Princess Grace Tel. 93.25.45.45 Fax. 93.50.84.85
One hundred rooms. 24-hour room service, valet parking, swimming pool, solarium, hairdresser, conference rooms, air conditioning.

The Mirebeau is the poor, neglected sister of the SBM hotel group. Architecturally uninspiring, it manages to be central without being convenient due to a convergence of busy roads around it.

Rooms are brightly decorated with modern furnishings, and most have a separate dressing room.

The Mirabeau's consolation is its restaurant "La Coupole," which rates a Michelin star. The decor is refined but, again, uninspired, in contrast to the excellent cuisine. The seven-course "Menu Gourmand," (which includes shrimp scampi marinated in basil oil) is 390 francs/$71.

Beach Plaza Hotel (MC) $$$
22 avenue Princess Grace. Tel. 93.30.98.80 Fax. 93.50.23.14
Three hundred and sixteen rooms. 24-hour room

service, valet parking, swimming pools, private beach, restaurant, piano bar, travel agency, car rental, shops, conference rooms.

Originally built as a ritzy Holiday Inn, it is now part of the British Forte Group. The Beach Plaza occupies a quiet niche on the far east end of Monte Carlo's coast, near the Sporting d'Ete entertainment complex.

A tranquil patio with open-air dining and a private beach, plus a recreation area and three pools (including a shallow children's pool), makes this hotel ideal for families.

The Sunday buffet brunch, all you can eat for 220 francs/$37.60, may be one of the best deals in town for those with a large appetite. Choose from a hot and cold buffet plus cheese and dessert, including crepe suzettes. Children half-price. 11:30-2:30.

THREE STAR

Abela Hotel (F) $$
23 avenue des Papalins. Tel. 92.05.90.00 Fax. 92.05.91.67
One hundred and ninety-two rooms. Restaurant, bar, parking garage, car rental, conference rooms, a non-smoking floor, and access to a pool.

The only hotel in Fontvieille, Monaco's new quarter. Essentially, a businessman's budget hotel, conveniently situated within several minutes' walk of the Heliport.

The Abela is clean, modern and attractively furnished; ideal for anyone wishing easy access to the Olympic Stadium and the Espace.

Hotel Alexandra (MC) $$
35 boulevard Princesse Charlotte. Tel. 93.50.63.13
Fifty-five rooms. Some rooms have air conditioning. Color television.

A central Monte Carlo location with basic rooms, simple furniture. Drab but clean.

Hotel Balmoral (MC) $$
12 avenue de la Costa. Tel. 93.50.62.37 Fax. 93.50.62.37
Seventy-seven rooms. Restaurant and bar, air conditioning, television.

The family-run Balmoral enjoys the same harbor views as the Hermitage. It is central, quiet and sunny. Room decoration is not impressive, but compensated by reasonable tariffs.

Apartments are available for 1,200 francs per night/$218.

Hotel du Louvre (MC) $$
16 boulevard des Moulins. Tel. 93.50.65.25
Thirty-four rooms. Air conditioning, color television, minibar.

Tucked into Monte Carlo's main shopping street, the recently-renovated Hotel du Louvre is, like Hotel Alexandra, the best deal for those who wish to be within easy reach of the Casino and the public beach at a moderate price.

Hotel Miramar (C) $$
1 avenue President J-F Kennedy. Tel. 93.30.86.48
Thirteen rooms. Pizzeria. Air conditioning. No
television.

Adjacent to the quay; ideal for boat-lovers. Every
room has a private terrace overlooking the port.

Hotel le Siecle (C) $$
10 avenue Prince Pierre. Tel. 93.30.25.56 Fax.
93.30.03.72
Thirty-five rooms. Restaurant, bar, air conditioning,
television.

Opposite the train station, this cheerful hotel is
one of Monaco's best values. It was completely
renovated in 1987 and the marble bathrooms, with
built-in hairdryers, are superb for its star rating. A
warm, cosy brasserie on the ground floor serves
meals and snacks.

Hotel le Versailles (C) $$
4 avenue Prince Pierre. Tel. 93.50.79.34
Fifteen rooms.

Nondescript but comfortable. Small pizzeria on
the ground floor.

TWO STAR

Hotel Terminus (C) $
9 avenue Prince Pierre. Tel. 93.30.20.70 Fax.
93.50.78.05
Fifty-four rooms.

Simple, sparse and cheap, the Terminus is adjacent to the train station, and its rooms vibrate accordingly.

A small cafe in front overlooks the station forecourt—one can watch the commuters arrive each morning over a cafe au lait.

Residence des Moulins (MC) $
27 boulevard des Moulins. Tel. 93.30.60.86
Ten rooms. No credit cards.

Extremely low profile, on the second-floor of an apartment building overlooking Monte Carlo's main shopping street. A rooming house feel, like a bed-and-breakfast, without the breakfast. Simply the lowest overnight price-tag in Monte Carlo.

ONE STAR

Hotel Helvetia (C)
1 bis rue Grimaldi. Tel. 93.30.21.71
Twenty-eight rooms.

Situated in the center of La Condamine's quaint shopping area, across the street from the open-air market.

Hotel de France (C)
6 rue de la Turbie. Tel. 93.30.24.64
Twenty-six rooms. Visa and Master Charge only.

One of the best bargains in town, near the train station on a narrow Condamine backstreet. While lacking amenities (no elevator), the Hotel de

France is clean and was redecorated in 1991. Not all rooms have private baths.

A ground floor suite can sleep five for only 700 francs/$127.

Hotel Cosmopolite (C)
4 rue de la Turbie. Tel. 93.30.16.95
Twenty-four rooms.

Clean and neat, but best suited for students and backpackers.

No elevator. Not all rooms have private baths.

YOUTH HOSTEL

Centre de la Jeunesse Princesse Stephanie (C)
24 avenue du Prince Pierre. Tel. 93.50.83.20
Sixty rooms.

A glamorous, privately-run youth hostel for those between 16-26 (or up to 30 with a student ID).

The rooms sleep four, the showers are pristine and it has a sunny garden with ping-pong tables. (A swimming pool may soon be added.)

In the summer, it operates on a first-come-first-served basis, doors open at 7:00 a.m., and there is a maximum three-night limit.

In winter, the maximum stay is five nights. Reservations are accepted and recommended.

Munching Out

*M*onaco bustles with restaurants: French brasseries and bistros, Italian pizzerias, creperies, seafood, and ethnic eateries, from Tex-Mex to Japanese. It is even possible to sample authentic Monegasque cuisine!

Gastronomes can savor the culinary delights of the three-star Louis XV while budget-conscious tourists can eat well in the family-run establishments frequented by Monegasques.

Simply stated, food in Monaco is delicious.

Watch the restaurateurs shop for their fresh meat and poultry, seafood, fruit and vegetables at the open-air market in La Condamine early each morning.

Farmers bring their products from the surrounding mountains, where almost everything is organically home-grown. You need only bite into a tomato—so sweet, you can eat it on its own—to discover natural flavor.

Restaurants in Monte Carlo tend to be more expensive than those in Monaco's other neighbor-

hoods, but some should not be missed, even if they cater to tourists.

On La Condamine's narrow streets one will discover charming neighborhood bistros.

In hot weather, get away from the hustle-bustle and down to Fontvieille harbor, where a handful of terraced restaurants bask in the cool sea breeze.

All told, there are many more than a hundred restaurants in the Principality.

We have selected 20 that are most likely to enhance your visit.

Note: *Tap water in Monaco is exceptionally clean, safe to drink and, in fact, quite delicious. Though some waiters may push mineral water, it is an unnecessary indulgence.*

Cafe de Paris (MC)
Place du Casino. Tel. 92.16.21.21
Open daily 8:00 a.m.-2:00 a.m.
Credit cards.

A staple. One of the best people-watching spots in the Principality. A brasserie of such versatility, you can start your morning here, over a croissant and cappucino in the open-air; you can enjoy lunch inside or out, perhaps a salad nicoise or canneloni; you can enjoy tea and home-made pastries in the late afternoon, as the sun dips behind the Hotel de Paris; you can dine in elegance all evening; or simply watch the beautiful people and the people watchers over an ice cream sundae.

Cafe de Paris is a focal point, and it is consistently delightful.

Rebuilt in 1988, the interior brasserie is decorated with glorious 19th century stained glass. This is where the "crepe suzette" was created at the turn-of-the-century.

The menu is eclectic; look for the daily specials; they are often superb.

Expensive. Reservations (for lunch and dinner) recommended.

Le Texan (C)
4 rue Suffren Reymond. Tel. 93.30.34.54
Open for lunch and dinner Monday-Friday; evening only Saturday; closed Sunday.
Credit cards.

As its name suggests, Le Texan is an American-style restaurant offering Tex-Mex chow "with a French flair." It is simply the most popular restaurant in Monaco.

This is the place where you are most likely to catch a glimpse of the young royals hanging out with their friends. Or Magic Johnson. Or Roger Moore. Whenever the stars are in town, they find Le Texan, and they return again and again.

Le Texan is also the social center for the young internationals who live in Monaco, and a second home to the students up and down the Cote d'Azur.

If you don't wish to eat, you can grab a stool (if you can find one) and "hang-out" with the locals at the long Alamo Bar. Tables are for diners, who munch-out on fajitas, chimichangas, tacos or, for the less daring, T-bone steaks and burgers.

Moderately priced. Reservations essential.

Le Louis XV (MC)

Hotel de Paris, Place du Casino. Tel. 93.25.59.17
Closed: Tuesday and Wednesday. Credit cards.

Monaco's only three-star restaurant, in the gilded dining room of the Hotel de Paris, is one of the most overwhelmingly luxurious restaurants in the world. Every detail is opulent, from the shimmering crystal to golden cutlery to black-tie waiters who whisk brocade footstools to each table for handbags. There is a 220,000-bottle wine cellar.

World-renowned Chef Alain Ducasse creates an inventive cuisine that calls on fresh Provencal herbs and bright Italian accents.

Very expensive. Plan to spend 1500 francs for two with wine.

Reservations mandatory.

Le Grill (MC)

Hotel de Paris, Place du Casino. Tel. 93.50.80.80
Open daily for lunch and dinner. Credit cards.

Atop the Hotel de Paris, The Grill Room is less formal than Louis XV, but every bit as chic. Superb grilled meat and fish in an impeccable oval blue-and-white dining room with views over the harbor. Try the souffle du Mandarin for dessert.

The Grill Room's ceiling slides open to the stars in fine weather.

Expensive. Reservations essential

Le Saint Benoit (MC)

10 avenue de la Costa. Tel. 93.25.02.34
Closed Monday. Credit cards.

Perhaps the finest seafood restaurant in the Principality. You can dine inside or on an open-air patio with a panoramic view of the harbor.

The local seafood specialty is the "Loup" (sea bass), grilled with Provencal herbs and olive oil. Go for it! (You won't be disappointed.)

Expensive. Reservations essential.

L'Off Shore (F)
22 quai Sanbarbani. Tel. 92.05.90.99
Closed Monday. Credit cards.

Small and sophisticated with a sleek and sporty hi-tech appearance. Halogene lamps, suspended from the ceiling, hang over each table, creating a futuristic intimacy.

Superb seafood and open-air dining on the harbor-front.

Expensive.

Pinnochio (MV)
30 rue Comte Felix Castaldi. Tel. 93.30.96.20
Closed Wednesday. Credit cards.

A charming restaurant of sheer magic, even if the tables are squeezed close together (outside seating in good weather). The home-made ravioli, with a choice of four sauces, may be the finest in Europe. The pasta is also excellent.

Afterwards, take a walk through The Rock, and enjoy a nighttime view of Monte Carlo, Roquebrune, Cap Martin and Menton from a scenic point near the Palace.

Reservations recommended.

Polpetta (MC)
2 rue Paradis. Tel. 93.50.67.84
Closed Saturday lunch. Credit cards.

Superb pasta and a warm, intimate atmosphere have made Polpetta the most popular Italian restaurant among those who live in Monaco. (It is off the beaten track, within inches of the French border, and most tourists can't find it). Rumored to be a favorite of Prince Rainier and Frank Sinatra. The complimentary home-made Grappa at meal's end is the best in Monaco.

Moderately-price. Reservations essential.

Le Michelangelo (F)
8 quai des Sanbarbani. Tel. 93.25.55.85
Closed Saturday lunch and Sunday. Credit cards.

The Pizza Michelangelo (with garlic sauce) and a "mesclun" salad on the open-air terrace beside the berthed yachts of Fontvieille harbor is a delightful experience.

Moderately priced. Reservations essential.

Rampoldi (MC)
3 avenue des Spelugues. Tel. 93.30.70.65
Open daily. Credit cards.

A high-profile landmark, and listed here for that reason, not the food. Reputed to be a favorite among celebs like Karl Lagerfeld, Princess Caroline, and Ringo Starr. People like to be seen here. Request the elevated right-hand side, where the insiders and celebrities are seated.

Expensive. Reservations essential.

Sam's Place (MC)
1 avenue Henri Dumant. Tel. 93.50.89.33
Open daily. Credit cards.

A fun, lively eatery near Hotel Hermitage. Ideal for a light meal after a movie or before a show. Simple cooking; best hamburgers in Monaco. The plat du jour is always superb.

Moderately priced. Reservations suggested.

Chez Bacco (C)
25 boulevard Albert 1er. Tel. 93.50.13.31
Closed Sunday. No credit cards.

Fine meat, fish and pasta in a friendly, intimate setting across from the port.

Le Perigordin (MC)
5 rue de Oliviers. Tel. 93.30.06.02
Closed Sunday. Credit cards.

A small, out-of-the-way bistro specializing in southeastern French cuisine. Many and varied duck dishes in a comfortable setting. The proprietor likes to practice his English and seems to adore Americans; he makes you feel like a guest in his home.

Inexpensive. Reservations recommended.

Trittico Doro (MC)
7 avenue Princesse Grace. Tel. 93.30.59.40.
Credit cards.

New to Monaco—a delightful new restaurant created by an Italian countess who loves to cook.
Moderate. Reservations suggested.

African King (C)
4 rue Langle. Tel. 93.50.97.02
Closed Saturday lunch, Sunday. Credit cards.

An Italian family pizza parlor, on a Condamine backstreet. Pizza dough is kneaded while you watch, then baked in a wood-fire brick oven. There's a bottle of hot-pepper oil, a local specialty, on each table. Try it on your pizza. The pasta is also excellent.
Inexpensive. Reservations not necessary.

Pizzeria Monagasque (C)
4 rue Terrazzani. Tel. 93.30.16.38
Open daily, dinner only. Credit cards.

Wood-burning pizza ovens warm the dining area on a brisk night. The setting is romantic and the pizza and other specialties scrumptious.

Fuji Maona (MC)
Summer: Sporting Club. Tel. 93.50.05.45
Winter: Galerie Metropole, Level II. Tel. 93.30.40.11
Closed Sunday, Monday lunch. Credit cards.

Monaco's only Japanese restaurant, complete with sushi bar and imported sushi chefs.

Chinatown (C)
11 bis, boulevard Rainier III. Tel. 93.30.30.61
Closed Monday. Credit cards.

The best of Monaco's three Chinese restaurants. Has seen finer days; indeed, it was once a regular haunt for Prince Rainier and Princess Grace.

Le Castelroc (MV)
Place du Palais. Tel. 93.30.36.68
Open for lunch only. Closed Saturday. Credit cards.

Authentic Monegasque cooking. For several generations, an old Monegasque family has served specialties like tender "barbaguian" turnovers filled with minced veal, local artichoke and a hint of garlic. Locals fill the place every Friday for the weekly "Stockofi," a traditional fish stew flavored with black olives, tomatoes and potatoes.

Le Castelroc faces the Palace and is the favorite lunchtime haunt of Palace staff.

Moderately priced. Reservations essential

Touline (F)
42 quai Sanbarbani. Tel. 92.05.28.20
Closed Sunday. Credit cards.

Good French country food along Fontvieille's peaceful port. The moules mariniere (mussels in garlic broth) and chicken liver salad are among the tasty appetizers, followed by tender steaks or fresh fish.

PUBS

Flashman's (MC)
7 avenue Princesse Alice. Tel. 93.30.09.03

The oldest English-pub in Monaco; an institution whose regulars should be institutionalized. "Flashman's proves that even Monaco has lowlife," says one well-bred wit. Noisy and rowdy. The restaurant in back serves diabolically bad English food. Good for singles, not much else.

The Ship and Castle (F)
42 Quai des Sanbarbani.

A local haunt for Fontvieille's English yachting crowd. Fish 'n' chips every Friday night; roast beef and Yorkshire pudding on Sunday.

Inexpensive. Sunday reservations recommended.

Le Snooker Pub (C)
6 rue Langle. Tel. 93.25.08.34
Open daily, 3:00 pm-3:00 a.m.

Good snacks. But aside from the pool room upstairs, doesn't quite know what it wants to be. What it is, is a "French-American, English pub-style" hangout, trendy among the young French.

Freaky Pub (MC)
7 rue du Portier. Tel. 93.25.87.67
Evenings. Closed Sunday

Young, hip, busy and beery. The closest thing to "beat" in Monaco.

Stars 'n' Bars (C)
6 rue Antoine 1st. Tel. 93.50.95.95
Day and night. Closed Monday.

Monaco's only Sports Bar. A full menu, including American deli-style sandwiches. Video-games, pinball machines and even a playroom for kids. TV monitors everywhere featuring international sporting events. American-style brunch on weekends.

Low Life—
High Life

Monaco on $50 a Day

ACCOMMODATION

Hotel de France

Hotel Helvetia

Hotel Cosmopolite

Residence des Moulins

It is possible to find a room in these hotels for under $25, but don't expect a color television or a private bath.

BREAKFAST

Skip the hotel breakfast. Treat yourself to a croissant and cafe au lait at one of the two arcade cafes in the open-air market at Places des Armes. About three dollars.

LUNCH

Buy a baguette (French bread), cheese and ham or pate, and a piece of fruit, from the marketeers, and pack yourself a picnic. You can go to the beach, or choose from many small parks for a place to spread out. About seven dollars.

Or buy a ready-made *pan bagnat*, a tasty sandwich on a French roll made with hard-boiled egg, tuna, tomato, onions, peppers, black olives, lettuce laced with olive oil and sprinkled with fresh basil—a local specialty.

DINNER

There are a handful of family-run brasseries in La Condamine that offer three course home-cooked meals at a *prix fixe* (fixed price) of 55 to 65 francs, about ten to twelve dollars.

Chez Saint Pierre
4 rue Baron-Sainte-Suzanne. Tel. 93.30.30.46

Santa Cruz
10 rue Terrazzani. Tel. 93.30.21.25

Le Lion D'Or
6 rue Imberty, Square Gastaud

Monte Carlo Bar
1 avenue Prince Pierre

Excellent pizza and pasta.

Le Dauphin Verte
20 rue Princesse Caroline

Lunch, not dinner (have your main meal at midday like the French; picnic at night).

Plat du jour, 45 francs. Changes each day. Typical Tuesday: Roast beef and mashed potatoes.

NIGHTLIFE

You still have five bucks—that'll buy three draft beers ("pression") at **Le Texan**.

And since there is no admission charge at **Jimmy'z**, you can boogie the night away for hours on the dance floor at no charge—as long as you don't sit down! (If you do, you are compelled to order a drink the price of tomorrow's budget.) Jacket and tie required.

Monaco on $5,000 a Day

This, too, can be done without exerting oneself.

ACCOMMODATION

Go for a suite at the **Hotel de Paris**. Not just *any* suite: Ask for 420, the one with the jacuzzi and magnificent view. Price tag: 11,200 francs/$2,036 per night.

LUNCH

The Grill Room, Hotel de Paris.

DINNER

Louis XV, Hotel de Paris.

SIGHTSEEING

Rent a Mercedes Silver Star (room for seven passengers) and a chauffeur from Monaco Limousine. Tel. 93.50.82.65

Cost: 280 francs/$50 an hour plus 11 francs/ $2 per kilometer or 600 francs/$110 an hour unlimited mileage.

SHOPPING

Let *their* legs do the walking. Monaco's merchants will come to *your* suite with a briefcase full of jewels.

And if you are looking for the ultimate souvenir for your kids: a scaled-down Ferrari, available at Ferrari Formula, 15 rue Grimaldi, La Condamine. Price: $10,000.

CRUISE

Rent a yacht and sail to Portofino and back, catered by Mister Brian, Monaco's ubiquitous society caterer.

A 65-foot vessel accomodating six passengers in three double cabins for $4,000 a day.

Or the 138-foot Jamaica Bay with a crew of eight for eight passengers (mahogany-paneled walls and luxurious dining room). Price: 352,200 francs/ $64,000 per week or 58,665 francs/$10,666 per day.

Camper and Nicholson (C), 11 boulevard Albert 1st. Tel. 93.50.84.86

Mister Brian (MC), 7 rue de Berceau. Tel. 93.30.50.09
Open: Monday-Saturday, 8:30 a.m. to 12:30 p.m. and 4:00 p.m. to 8:30 pm.

BEACHES

The only way to do this right is rent a cabana for the summer at the **Monte Carlo Beach Club**.

35,000 francs for the season ($6,350). Oh, you still have to pay for membership: 4,500 francs per person ($820).

A la carte membership: 145 francs per day ($26.50)–and if you want a mat, throw in another 75 francs ($13.50)

DAY TRIPPER

Take a helicopter from Monaco to St. Tropez in 25 minutes. Price: 4,260 francs/$775

Charter a helicopter to Milan (one hour and 20 minutes) for a shopping spree. Price: 15,200 francs/ $2,765

If you are coming to do Monaco extravagantly, you probably want to be here for a grand event:

- The Grand Prix and the Awards Gala on the final night, attended by Prince Rainier and his family. May. Inquiries: Automobile Club de Monaco Tel. 93.15.26.00.

- The Red Cross Gala. One of the most exclusive parties on earth; tickets are usually sold out a year in advance. First weekend in August. Inquiries: SBM (800) 221-4708.

- America in Monaco Week. July 4th weekend. A Texas-style open-air barbeque street party with live music and a celebrity softball game.

- Showboat International Rendezvous. A three-day event for the international yachting community. Prize yachts race; an awards ceremony follows. Activites are based around the Yacht Club de Monaco. July 4th weekend. Inquiries: Showboat International (305) 525-8626.

Sights

Monaco Ville/"The Rock"

It is here, in this genuine medieval village, that the relics of Monaco's history can be found. The narrow brick streets were not built with cars in mind and, consequently, most of The Rock is pleasantly pedestrian-oriented.

You get there by climbing the stone steps of the Rampe Major—200 feet—near Place des Armes, or by public bus. (Tip: Take the bus up; walk down).

The Princes' Palace

The Prince's stucco palace is perched daintily on ancient fortifications to the rear of The Rock. It is the official residence of the Grimaldis, Europe's oldest ruling family—the flag is raised whenever the Prince is in residence.

Constructed on the site of a 13th century Genovese fortress, it overlooks the whole of Monaco, and possesses a breathtaking view of the French coast into Italy.

The Hercules Gallery, overlooking the Court of

Honor, is where new-born heirs are presented to the Monegasques.

Tours of the Public Rooms are held daily, June through October, 9:30am to 6:30pm. Admission: 25 francs/$4.50.

Year round, catch a glimpse of court pageantry by observing the ceremonial Changing of the Guard. Daily at 11:55 a.m.

The Cathedral of Saint-Nicolas

Built in 1875 in a Romano-Byzantine style, the Church of Immaculate Conception houses the funeral chapels for the Grimaldis. Princess Grace is buried here.

From September to June, the Monaco Boys Choir sings at 10am Sunday mass.

The Oceanographic Museum

This is reputed to be the finest museum of its kind. Founded in 1910 by Prince Albert 1st, and directed by Jacques Cousteau for over 30 years, this active scientific center houses fossils, reproductions of early diving gear and oceanographic boats. The splendid basemet acquarium holds hundreds of colorful fish from the world over.

Exhibits are laid out in clear pictorial fashion, easy to understand, and there are electronic displays, along with a movie theatre.

Terrace restaurant on the roof.

Avenue Saint-Martin.

Open daily 9:00 a.m. to 7:00 p.m. (changes

seasonally). Admission: 50 francs/$9 (adults), 20 francs/$3.60 (children, students).

The Monte Carlo Story

A 35-minute slide show, screened eight times a day, in a small auditorium that traces the Grimaldis and the history of Monaco from the 13th century to the present.

Terrace du Parking des Pecheurs.

Open daily 11:00 a.m. to 5:30 p.m. Admission: 32 francs/$5.80 (adults), 15 francs/$2.70 (children).

The Historial (Wax Museum)

A musty collection of wax models, in 24 tableaus, that tells the history of the Grimaldi family. The period costumes are mostly reproduction.

For those particularly interested in Monaco's history or for wax museum devotees.

27 rue Basse. Open daily, 9:30 a.m. to 7:00 p.m. Admission: 20 francs/$3.60.

The Museum of Old Monaco

A small museum devoted to Monegasque folklore and artifacts.

Rue Emile de Loth. Summer: Monday-Wednesday-Friday, 2:30 p.m.-5:00 p.m.

Winter: Wednesday afternoons only. Admission: Free.

The Napoleonic Museum and the Palace Archives

This new wing of the Palace houses a collection of over one thousand Napoleonic mementos; the palace archives museum displays historic Monaco documents, uniforms of the Prince's Guard, and a complete set of Monegasque postage stamps and currency.

Place du Palais. Open daily, 10:30 a.m. to 12:30 p.m.; 2:00 p.m. to 5:00 p.m. Closed November. Admission: 15 francs/$2.70.

Monte Carlo

The glamourous Belle Epoque quarter where all the casino action takes place.

Place du Casino

Even if you don't gamble, the Monte Carlo Casino is a must to see. It is to Monaco what the Statue of Liberty is to New York City. Its green copper roof and delicate ceramic turrets define the Monaco skyline.

Designed by architect Charles Garnier (creator of the Paris Opera House), the opera house part of the Casino was inaugurated in 1879 with a poetry reading by Sarah Bernhardt, and it witnessed Nijinsky in some of his greatest roles. Today, the Monte Carlo Ballet performs here, as does Monaco's Philharmonic Orchestra and the Opera Company.

The Gaming rooms, with their gold borders, shimmering garlands and glimmering woodwork, are among the most impressive in the world; its artists renowned for their gilt complexes.

Casino Gardens

Take a leisurely walk through the picturesque gardens with fountains and sculpture chosen by Princess Caroline. A humongous Bottero sculpture of a black cat was orginally placed at the entrance to the Casino, but many gamblers complained, believing the cat would bring them bad luck, and it was moved across the square.

The National Museum of Fine Arts

This unique gallery houses an impressive collection of over 300 dolls and mechanical toys amassed by Madelaine de Galea, whose portrait by Pierre-Auguste Renoir hangs in the foyer.

The elaborately-coiffed 19th century fashion dolls were created by couturiers to promote their newest styles to wealthy clients.

The 80 mechanical toys were expensive conversation pieces for the European bourgeoisie in the 1800s, and many are quite remarkable.

There is a three-foot high clown that blinks kidskin eyes and does magic tricks; a monkey that smokes a cigarette.

17 avenue Princesse Grace.

Open daily. Summer: 10:00 a.m. to 6:30 p.m. Winter: 10:00 a.m. to 12:15 p.m. and 2:30 p.m. to 6:30 p.m. Admission: 24 francs/$4.35 (adults), 14 francs/$2.50 (children).

La Condamine

A bustling harborside neighborhood between The Rock and Monte Carlo.

The Open-Air Market

The fruit and vegetable and flower market at Place des Armes is a color-fest for the eyes, and one of the the best people-watching spots in the Principality. Here, you are watching not the other tourists and the Beautiful People, but the natives, the "real" people of Monaco, who bustle about, picking and choosing their daily supply of fresh food.

Pull up a chair at one of the two arcade cafes and soak up the ambience.

Then explore the recently-renovated indoor market at the far end. Several stalls serve hot *socca*, a chick-pea pancake, the local specialty.

Places des Armes. From early morning till just past noon, 365 days a year.

The Zoological Gardens
(Centre D'Acclimatation Zoologique)

A small, intimate yet surprisingly robust zoo carved into a side of the Rock, near Place des Armes.

In the space of 30 minutes, you'll see a lion, Bengal tigers and other wild cats, a rhinocerous, a hippopotamus, a reptile house, and an array of apes, including oranguatangs and chimpanzees.

Place du Canton. Tel. 93.25.18.31

March-May: 10:00 a.m. to 12:00 p.m. and 2:00 p.m. to 6:00 p.m.

June-September: 9:00 a.m. to 12:00 p.m. and 2:00 p.m. to 7:00 p.m.

October-February: 10:00 a.m. to 12:00 p.m. and 2:00 p.m. to 5:00 p.m.

Admission: Adults 20 francs/$3.60; children 10 francs/$1.80 (seven years and under, free).

The Port of Hercules

Monaco's deep-water harbor was first used by Phoenician sailors. Today it provides mooring for 500 ships, including the 150-foot yacht, Atlantis, owned by Greek shipping magnate Stavros Niarchos, anchored here nearly year-round.

Catamaran Monte Carlo

This glass-bottomed Catamaran offers one-hour tours of Monaco from the sea four times a day and occasionally at night.

Embarquement Quai des Etats-Unis. Tel. 92.16.15.15

Prices vary. One-hour tours: Adults 65 francs/$11.80, children 45 francs/$8.20.

SeaBus

A Disneyland-style 44-seat submarine that tours simulated shipwrecks, artificial reefs and the brilliantly-colored Mediterranean flora and fauna a hundred feet below sea level.

For information: Societe Monegasque de Tourisme Sous-Marin, 11 boulevard Albert 1st. Tel. 92.16.18.19

Admission: Adults 270 francs/$50.60, children 150 francs/$27.30.

The Church of Saint Devote

Monaco's patron Saint Devote was a young Corsican martyr who would not renounce her faith and was tortured to death by the Romans in the year 304.

When Devote's body was shipped to Africa for burial, a storm swelled in the Mediterranean. Legend has it that a dove arose from her mouth and guided the ship to the Monegasque coast. A small chapel was erected on the site, and the relics of Saint Devote, credited with miracles, were used to rouse the troops to victory whenever Monaco was attacked.

Local lore suggests that an unscrupulous pirate named Antinope tried to steal the relics and was stopped by Monegasques who burned the trader's barge. This event—a barge burning—is re-enacted every year on Saint-Devote Day, January 27th.

The current church at Place Saint-Devote was commissioned by Charles III.

Moneghetti

A level above La Condamine.

Jardin Exotique (Exotic Gardens)

Monaco's mild climate is an Eden for over 7,000 varieties of cactus. Some are a hundred feet high; others more than 140 years-old. The gardens adjoin the Moneghetti Grottos, a prehistoric cave filled with stalagtites and stalagmites.

Boulevard du Jardin Exotique. Open daily from 9:00 a.m.

Admission: Adults 29 francs/$5.30, children 14.50 francs/$2.60.

The Museum of Prehistoric Anthropology

This small museum near the exotic gardens houses a collection of fossils from 5000 to 500 BC.

Admission to Jardin Exotique includes the Museum.

Fontvieille

Literally means "new village" and was entirely built on land reclaimed from the sea. Most of Monaco's industry is housed in Fontvieille, along with a pleasant marina and a state-of-the-art sports complex with football stadium.

The yachting crowd find Fontvieille's harbor preferable to the Hercules Port because it is off the beaten track and better protected from the current.

The Princess Grace Rose Garden

In the center of Fontvieille, this fragrant oasis is a

living memorial to Princess Grace, a long-time garden enthusiast, in Monaco's most serene setting.

Over 3,500 rosebushes have been donated by the Princesses' admirers from around the world.

The bronze statue of Princess Grace was sculpted by Dutch artist Kees Verkade.

Open from dawn to dusk.

Seasonal

The Princes' Fair

For three weeks in **November**, the promenade along the harbor is transformed into an amusement park with bumper-cars, fun-houses, merry-go-rounds, space rides, cotton candy, caramel apples and shooting galleries. This carnival celebrates the Prince's Saint Day, more important in Monaco than one's birthday.

International Circus Festival

The first week of **February**. An all-star competition of top circus acts from around the world. Week-long with evening performances and matinees for children.

International Fireworks Festival

July and August. Pyrotechnics from seven countries take it in turn to produce awesome firework displays over Monaco's Hercules Harbor. The winner of this competition is bestowed the honor of putting on a firework show during Prince Rainier's birthday celebrations. Precise dates change each year; check in advance with the Monaco Tourist Office.

Kidstuff

Playgrounds

In Monte Carlo, the boardwalk on the public beach is a haven for children; they congregate here after school and on weekends to skateboard and rollerskate.

On the Rock, **Saint Martin Gardens**, on a level below the Palace, overlooking Fontvieille Harbor. Ideal for toddlers.

In Fontvieille, **Jardin d'Enfants**, tucked in between the Princess Grace Rose Garden and the circus tent. Again, toddlers.

In Moneghetti, **Park Princesse Antoinette**, which also has miniature golf April 15 to October 15, Tuesday through Sunday, 2:00 p.m. to midnight.

In La Condamine, the promenade along the harbor is popular with kids. The open-air cafes have electronic games and foosball, and there is a colorful carousel year-round near the swimming pool. During the summer, two mini-trains—The Azur Express—run tourists on sightseeing trips along the promenade. One goes to the beach at Monte Carlo; the other, up to The Rock. Both return to the promenade. 17 francs; children three and under go free.

The Oceanographic Museum, the Galea Collection of dolls and toys and the zoo are generally a big hit with kids, as is the new Seabus submarine ride.

Ice Cream Parlors

Haagen Daz *(MC)*
Inside the Sporting d'Hiver and an open-air terrace around the corner, overlooking Casino Gardens.

La Casa del Gelato *(F)*
42 quai des Sanbarbani. Rich Italian ice cream. Count your change!

Toy Stores

Fantasio *(MC)*
19 boulevard des Moulins.

  The largest selection of toys in the Principality.

Au Royaume des Jouets *(C)*
14 rue Princesse Caroline.

  Barbies to Beachballs.

Nightlife

*D*espite its tiny size, Monaco has a varied nightlife. We offer four styles, elements of which can be inter-changed to suit your personality. Or why not try all four during the course of a week?

Unlike New York, where fashionable nightspots can sprout overnight then fade into oblivion at whim, the gears of trendiness grind slowly in Monaco. Jimmy'z, for instance, has always been THE nightclub.

"Monte Carlo Classic"

Start off with cocktails at the **American Bar** in the Hotel de Paris, once the haunt of David Niven and Greta Garbo. Mixed drinks cost about 50 francs/$9.

Dinner at **The Grill Room**, Hotel de Paris.

Or...

A dinner show in the **Salles des Etoilles** at the entertainment complex known as the Sporting d'Ete. The seasonal line-up often includes Shirley

MacLaine, Frank Sinatra, Diana Ross and Jerry Lewis. The ceiling slides open to an all-star supporting cast. Dinner is not mandatory; it is possible to go for drinks and the show. July and August only. The rest of the year, find rhinestone-studded cabaret (song and dance) in the Casino complex. Tel. 93.30.71.71.

The Casino. Head for the Private Rooms, 50 francs/$9 more than the standard entry fee; no charge with an SBM Gold Card.

Cafe de Paris. Place du Casino especially bustles with activity between midnight and 2:00 a.m. Take a front-row seat and a nightcap.

Formal dress recommended.

"Monaco Cool"

The only choice for apertifs and dinner: **Le Texan**. Turn up at about 8:30 p.m. for a 9:30 reservation. This gives you an hour at the Alamo Bar bar to savor margaritas, the local characters and a sculpted reproduction of The Alamo behind the bar. People are friendly and everyone speaks English.

When you phone to book a reservation, be sure to request a table on the covered terrace.

11:30 is still too early for Jimmy'z, so the Monaco Coolest cool their heels upstairs at **Stars 'n' Bars, The Blues Bar**, for live music and cocktails. 90 franc admission/$15.00 includes your first drink.

At midnight, not before: **Jimmy'z** (pronounced Jimmy's; not Jimmy Zs, truly uncool).

Valet parking only for celebrities or unknowns driving Ferraris or Lamborghinis.

There is no admission charge, but admission can be a problem during the summer if you are not young and beautiful. Inside tip: Say there is a bottle inside with your name on it. This will identify you as "insider" and doors will open. Insiders traditionally "invest" in a bottle and return to it over several nights.

A single drink, whether it's soft or hard, costs about 240 francs/$40. A bottle of vodka is 1400 francs/$255 and a bottle of champagne is priced at 1600 francs/$290.

The disco music is dated and many patrons are middle-aged, if young at heart. The roof opens in summer and the disco backs onto a lagoon.

The coolest of them all party and dance till 5:00 a.m., then head to **The Tip Top Club** for breakfast.

Jimmy'z (MC): Sporting d'Ete, 26 avenue Princesse Grace. Tel. 92.16.22.77

Stars 'n' Bars (C): 6 rue Antoine 1st. Tel. 93.50.95.95.

Tip Top Club (MC): avenue des Speluges. Tel. 93.30.69.13

Dress: Bluejeans and cowboy boots for Le Texan; a blazer or sport coat for Jimmy'z. The result is the Monaco Cool look: Jacket & jeans with elegant accessories.

"Las Vegas Monaco"

No need to leave **Loews**.

Cocktails at the groundfloor **Piano Bar**.

Dinner and floorshow at the **Folie Russe**, a cabaret combining creative dance numbers (many topless) and magic acts. The show starts at 11:00 p.m. Closed Monday.

Hit the tables—blackjack, craps, roulette—and the numerous slots.

Dress: Informal.

"Pizza and a Movie"

Practiced regularly by many Monaco residents.

Early evening drinks at **Le Texan**.

Pizza or pasta at a pizzeria in the low-profile Condamine neighborhood... **African King** or **Pizza Monegasque**.

Summer Cinema (MC), 26 avenue Princesse Grace. Tel. 93.25.86.80

Watch American movies in their original English beneath the stars in comfortable chairs with tables. Pay a little more for the canopied section in back. It has a bar for refreshment (plus ice cream and popcorn), and the ambience of a garden party. The main attraction starts at nightfall, about 9:30. Price: 50 francs/$9. From June 5th to September 30th.

Cinema Le Sporting (MC), Sporting d'Hiver, Place du Casino. Tel. 93.30.81.08

Year-round indoor cinema. American movies in their original English (called VOs, for "version originale"), are shown on Monday and Thursday (6:00 p.m. and 9:00 p.m.).

Dress: Casual. Price: 41 francs (30 francs for the early show).

Other Nightclubs

The Living Room (MC), 7 avenue des Speluges. Tel. 93.50.80.31

Quiet and more laid back than Jimmy'z. Favored by businessmen and divorced women; an older crowd 40-60. But also an after-show hangout for the dancing girls of the Folie Russe. No cover. 600 francs/$110 for a bottle of vodka; 900 francs/$165 for champagne. Light snacks available.

Le Noroc (MC), 7 rue du Portier. Tel. 93.25.09.25

Disco-dancing in a quiet, uncrowded environment. Dark and private, and very friendly service. Diverse in age. Singers welcome to accompany the pianist.

Le Tiffany's (MC), 3 avenue des Speluges. Tel. 93.50.53.13

Young and trendy.

Le Boccaccio (MC), 39 avenue Princesse Grace. Tel. 93.30.15.22

A smokey basement disco. This is where Monaco's croupiers hang-out.

A View of Monaco

The views from within Monaco are, of course, fabulous. But the only way to see ALL of Monaco is to get OUT of Monaco, and then the views become spectacular.

Head for the hills, toward old Rocquebrune, and stop for a drink at the Vista Palace Hotel. Floor to ceiling picture windows offer a breathtaking, panoramic view of Monaco to Menton, and the Italian coast beyond. Perfect at dusk as Monaco slowly lights up.

Then onto Rocquebrune, a charming medieval town perched on the side of a mountain, overlooking the Principality. The castle in Rocquebrune is said to be the oldest castle in France.

*For a truly authentic Provencal dinner, **La Dame Jeanne**. The building dates back to the 10th century. A romantic dinner for two runs about 500 francs/$90.*

La Dame Jeanne, 1 Chemin de Sainte Lucie, Rocquebrune-Village
Tel. 93.35.10.20. No credit cards.

L'X Club (MC), 13 avenue des Speluges. Tel. 93.30.70.55

Extremely young, French and casual—blue jeans. An 18-to-22 local disco crowd.

Pastimes

*C*hances are, you have come to Monaco for some recreation and relaxation. And whether your favorite pastime is gambling or bronzing yourself, working out or spectator sports, you have come to the right place. Monaco is THE place for self-indulgence.

People Watching

- Le Texan
- Cafe de Paris
- The open-air market at Place des Armes
- At one of several open-air cafes along the port-front (May through October).

Gambling

The Monte Carlo Casino (MC), Place du Casino. Tel. 92.16.21.21

The public gaming rooms open at noon (the slot machine room at 2:00 p.m.) every day of the year;

they close when the last players leave, usually between 2:00 and 4:00 a.m.

Proper dress required (no T-shirts or torn jeans). No one under 21.

Admission: 50 francs/$9. Weekly passes: 120 francs/$22. Monthly passes: 350 francs/$64. Admission free for guests of SBM hotels.

The Salons Privee (private rooms) open at 4:00 p.m. Admission: Another 50 francs/$9 (free for guests of SBM hotels).

SBM—Loews Casino (MC), Loews Hotel, 12 avenue des Speluges. Tel. 92.16.21.24

Open daily, year round, Monday to Friday from 5:00 p.m., weekends from 4:00 p.m. (Slot machines open at 11:00 a.m.)

Admission is free.

Le Cafe de Paris (MC), Place du Casino. Tel. 92.16.21.25

At the rear of the cafe's shopping complex, a small, casual casino.

Open every day, slot machines from 10:00 a.m., tables from 5:00 p.m.

Monte Carlo Sporting Club (MC), avenue Princesse Grace. Tel. 93.30.71.71

July to mid-September, every night from 10:00 p.m.

Public Beaches

The Larvotto

Monaco's sole public beach, adjacent to avenue Princesse Grace in Monte Carlo, is man-made of compressed sand.

Vendors offer umbrella and beach chair rentals, along with floats and dinghies.

The marble boardwalk is popular with joggers and children, for whom a skateboard ramp has been constructed.

Plage de la Mala

In nearby Cap d'Ail, adjacent to Fontvieille. A French beach popular among Monaco's residents to hide out from the tourists at the Larvotto.

NOTE: Opinions differ about the cleanliness of Monaco's Mediterranean beach water. Monaco has NOT been effected by recent oil spillages, but some doctors, citing a high bacteria count in the water, recommend showering after a dip in the sea. The best advice is: exercise caution.

Swimming Pools

Piscine des Terrasses (C)

2 avenue de Monte Carlo. Tel. 93.30.22.55.

Open daily, 9:00 a.m. to 8:00 p.m.

A heated (82 F) seawater pool, with outdoor solarium, run by SBM and available to SBM hotel guests.

This pool services the Hotel de Paris and the

Hermitage Hotel (connected by a marble tunnel), and is open to the public for a fee.

Admission, including towel, shower and dressing cabin: 70 francs/$13.

Light refreshment on the premises.

Stade Nautique Rainier III (C)
Quai Albert 1st. Tel. 93.15.28.75
An open-air heated seawater pool on the harbor.
Admission: 17 francs/$3.

Centre Nautique Prince Hereditaire Albert (F)
Stade Louis II, 2 avenue du Prince Hereditaire Albert. Tel. 93.15.42.13.

Open weekdays: 7:30 a.m. to 2:30 p.m., Saturday: 2:00 p.m. to 6:00 p.m., Sunday: 9:00 a.m. to 1:00 p.m.

Closed Wednesday; closed the month of August.

Admission: 15 francs/$2.75. Swimming lessons available: 50 francs/$9.

An Olympic-size freshwater pool in the sports stadium.

Gyms

Columbia Tonus Centre (MC)
7 avenue Princesse Grace. Tel. 93.25.03.27.

Nautilus equipment, aerobics and stretch classes, UVA tanning massage, beauty services, sauna, jacuzzi and a snack bar.

Admission: 120 francs/$22. Weekly membership is available at a more reasonable price.

Guy Mierczuk Center (C)
Quai Albert 1st. Tel. 93.30.23.35.

Monaco's hard-core iron-pumping gym is presided over by muscleman Guy Mierczuk, a former Mr. Universe and licensed osteopath-chiropractor.

Weight-training, aerobics, jazzercize, UVA tanning and a variety of esthetic treatments.

Admission: 55 francs/$10. Monthly pass: 350 francs/$63.50.

Health Spa—Loews
Look under Loews Hotel in *Sleeping Around*.

Hiking

Seaside Hikes:

1. From Monte Carlo Beach to Cap Martin—a quaint path that hugs the coastline.
2. From Plage de la Mala (the beach at Cap d'Ail) to Eze—a rugged cliffside path.

Golf

Monte Carlo Golf Club
Mont Agel. Tel. 93.41.09.11

A technical 18-hole par 71 course located high above Monaco and the ancient village of La Turbie, 20 minutes from the Principality. The setting is magical: 2500 feet above sea level with gorgeous mountain and sea views.

Though a private club, guests at SBM hotels enjoy membership privileges.

All others, with presentation of a golf handicap card: 300 francs/$54.50 weekdays, 400 francs/ $72.75 weekends.

Tennis

Monte Carlo Country Club
avenue de la Princesse Grace, Roquebrune-Cap Martin. Tel. 93.78.20.45.

A 23-court club adored by the pros and the stars, who come in droves every year to play the celebrity tournament. This is where Bjorn Borg staged his comeback in 1991.

Founded in 1928, the Club has 1300 members (and a long waiting list of hopefuls willing to pay a 35,000 franc entrance fee).

Guests of SBM hotels are permitted free access. Admission for all others: 250 francs.

Tennis Club of Monaco (MC)
29-29 boulevard de Belgique. Tel. 93.30.01.02.

A small private club that permits admission to non-members.

100 francs per person per hour.

Sailing

Sailing in Monaco revolves around the exclusive Monaco Yacht Club. While the Yacht Club's facilities and sponsored races are private, reciprocal privileges exist with many international yacht clubs.

For further information, contact the Yacht Club de Monaco.
Quai Antoine 1st. Tel. 93.50.58.39.

Windsurfing & Waterskiing

The Monte Carlo Beach Club (93.78.21.40), the Beach Plaza Sea Club (93.30.98.80) and the Ski Vol at Larvotto Beach (93.50.86.45) are water sporting centers.

Spectator Sports

The Louis II Stadium

Inaugurated in 1985, this immense sports complex hosts professional football (soccer) games in its 20,000-seat arena. Swimming and athletic meets, professional boxing matches and European basketball all take place in this Olympic stadium.

Louis II Stadium (F), 2 avenue Prince Hereditaire Albert. Tel. 93.15.40.00

Arts & Culture

Ballet

The Ballets de Monte-Carlo, rejuvenated by Princess Caroline in 1985, produces four productions a year, often original works. The Ballet is in residence November and December, March and April, and August. For ticket information call: 93.50.69.31

Drama

Major European dramatic productions are performed in Monaco, October through June. Most shows are in French.

Theatre Princesse Grace (MC), avenue d'Ostende. Tel. 93.25.32.27

The local English Language Drama Group performs at The Fort Antoine Theatre on summer evenings. It is an open-air ampitheatre on The Rock.

The Fort Antoine Theatre (MV), avenue de la Quarentaine. Tel. 93.15.80.00

Literature

The Irish Library houses Princess Grace's personal collection of rare Irish literary and musical editions.

In recent years, the library has made its reputation as a research facility for post-graduate students and professors, offering a lecture series and occasional seminars.

Directed by Professor Georges Sandoluscko.

By appointment only.

Princess Grace Irish Library (MV), 9 rue Princesse Marie de Lorraine. Tel. 93.50.12.25

Music

Monaco's Philhamonic Orchestra, founded in 1863, has been directed by Toscanini, Richard Strauss, Loenard Bernstein and Lorin Maazel. It performs regularly in the Congress Center Auditorium and the Salle Garnier, January through March.

Several times each summer, the Philharmonic performs under the stars in the Palace courtyard, the Court d'Honneur.

L'Orchestre Philharmonique de Monte Carlo (MC), Centre de Congres Auditorium. Tel. 93.50.76.54

Jazz on the Jetty—Each Sunday evening in August, a live jazz band performs on the harbor's north jetty. About 9:00 p.m. Free.

Shops

*I*t should come as no surprise that the emphasis, in Monaco, is on luxury goods. Where else could a sunny Mediterranean climate support four designer furriers?

Most of the fanciest shops (Cartier, Louis Vuitton, Chanel) are clustered around Place du Casino, the Temple of Big Spending.

For rainy-day shopping, Monaco has three suitably upscale malls. The most elegant, Galerie du Metropole, with its marble floors, crystal chandeliers and grand staircases, probably belongs in our chapter on sightseeing. The elegant, smaller, Galerie du Sporting d'Hiver, is a stone's throw away from the Place du Casino.

This being the Mediterranean, most shops close at 12:30 p.m. for lunch and reopen at 2:30 p.m.

NOTE: American citizens are entitled to tax refunds of about 16 percent on purchases over 1200 francs. It can make a big difference on high-ticket items. Some stores are willing to deduct the amount upon making a sale; others insist on *completing paperwork that is filed with French Customs upon departure.*

Art and Antiques

Sotheby's and **Christie's**, the international auctioneers, hold weekend sales in October, December, April and June, specializing in Old Master paintings, antique French furniture and classic automobiles.

Gallery B5 is on the cutting edge of the Grafitti Movement and the evolving modern art scene.

Among the 55 galeries in the Principality, **Adriano Ribolzi**'s shop is known for 17th and 18th century French furniture and Italian paintings from the 14-18th centuries. **Galerie 41** sells rare Chinese objects d'art and French 18th century furniture.

Monaco Fine Arts specializes in 19th and 20th century paintings. Often they have a small Renoir and an Eduard Cortes or two in stock. They regularly hold exhibitions of established living artists, including Duane Alt from California and Kees Verkade, a Dutch sculptor whose work graces Monaco's parks.

Pierre Nouvion is a dealer of contemporary paintings and sculpture.

Galerie Touraj always stocks an eclectic collection of twentieth century French paintings.

If the truth be known, the emphasis is on quality, not bargains. The Provence countryside, within striking distance of Monaco, is the place for antique collectors and bargain-hunters.

Sotheby's (MC), Sporting d'Hiver, Place du Casino. Tel. 93.30.88.80

Christie's (MC), avenue Saint Michel. Tel. 93.25.19.33

Adriano Ribolzi (MC), 6 avenue des Beaux Arts. Tel. 93.30.06.25

Galerie 41 (MC), 41 boulevard des Moulins. Tel. 93.50.74.38

Monaco Fine Arts (MC), Sporting d'Hiver. Tel. 93.50.74.38

Artis Monte-Carlo (MC), 1 Impasse de la Fontaine. Tel. 93.25.63.00

Galerie Pierre Nouvion (MC), 3 avenue de l'Hermitage. Tel. 93.25.70.75.

Galerie Touraj (MC), 17 avenue des Spelugues. Tel. 93.50.24.23

Gallery B5 (F), Le Grand Large, quai Sanbarbani. Tel. 92.05.91.20

Books

Scruples (C), 9 rue Princesse Caroline. Tel. 93.50.43.52.
   This English-run bookstore is the only shop in Monaco for English-language bestsellers, classics, pulps and children's books.

Centre Commercial, Fontvieille

The Principality's first real shopping center opened in late 1992. It hosts Carrefour, an American-style supermarket, and approximately 40 shops, including stylish boutiques offering a wide range of goods, from clothing and jewelry to home furnishings and CDs.

Monaco's only McDonald's is to be found in this state-of-the art shopping mall, albeit without their famous golden arches, which were considered inappropriate for the Principality.

Also to be found in the Centre Commercial is a vintage car museum, perhaps one of the world's best, featuring Prince Rainier's extensive and impressive private collection.

The center has created an easy transition for pedestrians wishing to reach Fontvieille.

Clothes

Finely tailored resortwear and evening dress are featured in most store windows. Many top European stylists have signature boutiques in Monaco: Chanel, Givenchy, Dior, Celine, Hermes, Yves Saint Laurent and Louis Vuitton are clustered around Place du Casino. Mila Schon, Escada and Sonia Rykiel are nearby. Stephane Kelian and Charles Jourdan also have shopfronts in Monaco.

For men, the clothing of Faconnable and Old River set the fashion scene in Monaco.

Charles Jourdan (MC), 18 boulevard des Moulins. Tel. 93.50.86.51

Dior Furs (MC), avenue des Beaux Arts. Tel. 93.30.79.78

Escada (MC), 27 avenue de la Costa. Tel. 93.30.51.61

Faconnable (MC), 23 boulevard des Moulins. Tel. 93.50.50.66

Givenchy (MC), avenue des Beaux Arts. Tel. 93.25.34.04

Hermes (MC), 11 avenue de Monte Carlo. Tel. 93.50.64.89

Louis Vuitton (MC), 6 avenue des Beaux Arts. Tel. 93.25.13.44

Mila Schon (MC), 7 boulevard des Moulins. Tel. 92.16.08.07

Old River (MC), 17 boulevard des Moulins. Tel. 93.50.33.85

Sonia Rykiel (MC), 3 avenue Princesse Grace. Tel. 93.25.83.70

Stephane Kelian (MC), 3 rue Grimaldi. Tel. 93.30.14.59

Yves Saint Laurent (MC), avenue des Beaux Arts. Tel. 93.25.01.32

Pollini (MC), 3 boulevard des Moulins. Tel. 93.50.50.13

DISCOUNT DESIGNER CLOTHING:

La Difference (MC), 3 avenue Saint-Charles. Tel. 93.50.61.57

An unlikely shop, but nonetheless, run out of a cellar in the heart of Monte Carlo. Genuine designer fashions for men and women at rock-bottom wholesale prices.

Food & Wine (Gourmet Goodies)

Au Grand Echanson (MC) is an elegant wine store. 32 boulevard des Moulins. Tel. 93.50.61.19

Maison du Caviar (MC) operates a small caviar-blini restaurant that packages its goodies for retail sale. 1 avenue Saint-Charles. Tel. 93.30.80.06

Mister Brian (MC) Mister Brian set up shop in Monaco when he discovered that Scotch smoked salmon was unavailable in the Principality. His shop stocks smoked salmon and a host of other goodies imported from Britain and the USA. 7 avenue Berceau. Tel. 93.30.50.09.

Gifts

Boutique du Rocher (MC and MV) is a showcase for Monegasque craftsmen: hand-made ceramics, toys, beautifully embroidered children's clothes and scarves with motifs designed by Princess Grace, who founded this delightful pair of shops. 1 avenue de la Madone and 11 rue Emile de loth. Tel. 93.30.91.17

G.J.3 (MC) is a wonderful gift shop in the galerie

du Sporting d'Hiver. Silver frames, umbrellas, canes, elegant gambling paraphernalia—a serendipity of gifts for any occasion. Galerie du Sporting d'Hiver, avenue Princesse Alice. Tel. 93.25.55.11

Aux Ramparts du Vieux Monaco (MV) features ceramic miniatures of Provencal villages by local artist Jean-Pierre Gault. 17 rue Basse. Tel. 93.25.59.59

Services

Car Rental

Avis (C), 9 avenue d'Ostende. Tel. 93.30.17.53

Europcar (MC and F), The Heliport. Tel. 93.50.16.36; 47 avenue de Grande-Bretagne. Tel. 93.50.74.95

Hertz (C), 27 boulevard Albert 1st. Tel. 93.50.79.60

Tuxedo Rental

Jacques Bourdin (C), 5 rue Princesse Caroline. Tel. 93.30.49.22

Mag Deux (MC), Boulevard de France. Tel. 93.50.83.42

Hair Dressers (Unisex)

Jacques Dessanges (C), 31 rue Grimaldi. Tel. 93.50.23.67

Jean Louis David (MC), Galerie du Metropole. Tel. 93.50.30.60

Formule One sells Ferrari knick-knacks: key rings, wrist-watches, money-clips, driving jackets.

Texan Trading Post (C) T-shirts, just like the bartenders wear, have become Monaco's best-selling souvenir. They are on sale, along with other Le Texan accessories and Tex-Mex artifacts, at this new boutique adjacent to Le Texan. Tee shirts are priced 70 francs/$12.75. 6 rue Suffren Reymond.

Jewelers

Always near the casinos, these glittery shop-front windows tempt casino winners to buy shiny baubles for their loved ones.

Repossi (MC) exclusively sells Monaco Yacht Club and Golf Club accessories: watches, tie-pins and cufflinks. Square Beaumarchais. Tel. 93.50.89.59

Cartier (MC), Place du Casino. Tel. 93.30.86.58

Fred (MC), Loews Hotel. Tel. 93.30.79.00

Van Cleef & Arpels (MC), Place du Casino. Tel. 93.50.54.08

Bulgari (MC), avenue des Beaux-Arts. Tel. 93.50.88.40

Tabbah (MC), 21-23 avenue de Monte Carlo. Tel. 93.50.22.02

Wurz (MC), Place du Casino. An up-market pawn shop with a sparkling array of second-hand jewelry, presumably lost to the tables.

The Grand Prix

*M*onaco's Grand Prix is the most prestigious Formula One racing competition in the world.

Each spring, usually in May, over 100,000 visitors descend upon the Principality for its premier sporting event.

The Grand Prix course has changed little since its debut in 1929. The two-and-one-half mile circuit begins in La Condamine, by the harbor, and swerves right, up a hill toward Monte Carlo, through Place du Casino, loops around past Loews, and runs along the sea back to the harbor.

The Principality pulses with suspense as the 26 race cars zoom 74 to 78 laps in two hours through city streets, tackling hairpin turns, engines revving at maximum RPMs. Maneuvering is everything in this race; skill counts more than speed. A victory at Monte Carlo is every race-driver's dream.

The Monaco Automobile Club faces a formidable task year each to set up the circuit. It takes six weeks to resurface the roads, construct barriers and erect bleachers and grandstands.

There is enormous demand for the 34,000 available seats on the circuit; even greater demand for restaurant seating and hotel rooms with a view of the action.

Henry Ford II leased whole sections of the Hotel de Paris every year for public relations galas.

The Grand Prix runs concurrently with the nearby Cannes Film Festival; celebrities, like Paul Newman, often come to the Riviera for both events.

Prince Rainier watches the race from the Royal Box at the start and finish line, then retreats to a private party in an apartment with a commanding view of the action.

Ordering Tickets

The Monaco Automobile Club is the main source of Grand Prix tickets.

They mail ticket order forms on November 5th, six months before the race, to everyone on their mailing list. To get on their mailing list, simply write them:

> Automobile Club de Monaco
> 23 boulevard Albert 1st
> MC 98000 Monaco

Upon processing your order form and payment, the club dispatches your tickets by registered mail.

Tickets are also available through special kiosks in Monaco during the weeks preceding the big race.

Prices

From 450 francs/$80 (standing) to 1100 francs/$220 (seat with a good view).

Hotels

It is extremely difficult to find a hotel with Grand Prix vacancies; year-to-year bookings account for full houses everywhere. And even if you find a hotel, you must participate in a five-night "package" at prices two or three times the normal rate.

As a possible solution, you might try to find a hotel in Nice or Menton, and train in. Do NOT attempt to drive into Monaco on a race day.

Note: Many residents of Monaco rent out their apartments for Grand Prix week. Be prepared to part with about $10,000 for such a rental with a view. Look for these rentals in the classified ads of the *International Herald Tribune*, January through April.

Hanging with the Pit Crews

Monaco is a likely place to rub shoulders with Formula One drivers any time of the year. Ayton Senna, Nelson Piquet and Michele Alboreto all have homes in the Principality.

During Grand Prix week, race drivers, crews, mechanics and sportswriters gather at a few traditional party spots. Monte Carlo is popular with the racing set because it is the only Formula One race with a "free night" to socialize in the midst of hectic schedules. On Thursday night, find the grease crowd at these two down and dirty watering holes:

Rosie's Bar (MC) 11 avenue d'Ostende. Tel. 93.50.58.03

Rosie has been pouring draft beer from behind her bar for over 40 years. She knew most of the great drivers in the days when drivers drank and brawled with equal voracity.

Rosie's walls are plastered with Grand Prix memorabilia (including a steering wheel), and mementos from navy and merchant marine ships. The Rock supposedly tolerates this bar in the hope that sailors who stop in on their way up the hill to the Casino will get drunk here, not there, and go no further.

Tip-Top Bar (MC) Avenue des Speluges. Tel. 93.50.69.13

Graham Hill used to duck out of the Palace Award Galas to knock back brew with fellow racing cronies at Tip-Top, a hole-in-the-wall bar tucked in between the more refined establishments of avenue des Speluges. It remains a popular hang-out among racing insiders.

The Future of Monaco

With its small size, booming economy and progressive government, Monaco has been able to make rapid strides toward the year 2000, always taking the ecological environment into account.

New Train Station

Monaco has employed imaginative solutions to its most pressing problem: lack of territory. Having successfully reclaimed nine acres (one-seventh of Monaco's land area) from the sea through the Fontvieille project, Monaco is presently engaged in relocating its train station and railroad tracks to a subterranean setting.

The new underground station complex, expected to open in 1996, will include new shops and cafes.

It is a one billion franc-plus project—entirely financed by Monaco—and it will add three precious acres of land to the Principality.

New Pier

Monaco's Port de Hercules is the deepest harbor along the Cote d'Azur. It was considered bold and innovative when, in 1911, its two jetties with lighthouses were built in water 50-feet deep, under the supervision of Prince Albert 1st.

Eighty years later, a new pier has been designed to protect Monaco's port from southeast winds and uncomfortable currents. More than a jetty, it is expected to protrude straight out from Quai Antoine, at the base of the Rock, creating over 90,000 square feet of offices and apartments on seven floors.

Scheduled for construction in late 1993, sections of the pier will be pre-fabricated in a shipyard swimming pool then lifted by cranes and positioned in the sea.

In addition to new shops and restaurants, the pier will house a Cruiser Station, equipped to berth two 700-foot cruise ships, with waiting rooms, bars and other amenities one might expect to find at an airport or train station.

Sporting D'Ete

Monaco's entertainment complex will be given a facelift in the early '90s. A 400-room luxury seafront hotel and casino is planned.

Cultural Exhibition Center

A Cultural Exhibition Center on the avenue Princesse Grace in Monte Carlo is scheduled to open in 1998. Monaco hopes this center will attract major trade shows from around the world.

Transportation

Automobile traffic—estimated to increase by five percent each year—takes both a logistical and environmental toll on the Principality. There are proposals to establish an ambitious subterranean transportation system, a subway train, that would abolish most motor traffic and transform Monaco into a pedestrian zone. Visitors would park their cars at multi-level car parks at Monaco's border, to create a virtually car-free society. (Only cars with Monegasque registration plates and commercial delivery vehicles would be permitted access to Monaco's streets.)

Based on the Paris Metro, station stops would be built every 600 feet.

Another possibility under consideration is a monorail system, specifically designed to shuttle tourists to attractions throughout the Principality.

Ecology

Researchers at Monaco's Oceanographic Museum have recently developed the world's first living, self-sustaining laboratory coral reef. This innovation may lead to far-reaching ecological advances for our planet. Coral also has new applications in medicine.

Fontvieille II

After years of considering plans calling for "floating islands" in Monaco's sea space, the Principality's public works department has decided that the most realistic way to create more territory is to expand Fontvieille: Fontvieille II.

It is thought that early in the 21st century Monaco will endeavor to double Fontvieille's current size. The plan calls for an enlargement of Monaco's busy heliport and the construction of an airport to accommodate small to mid-size aircraft.

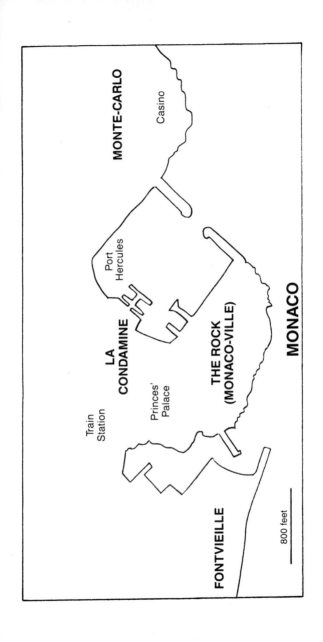

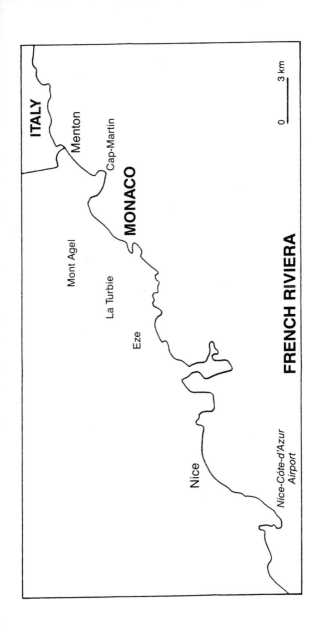